Weather Watch

Rain

by Jenny Fretland VanVoorst

Bullfrog Books

Ideas for Parents and Teachers

Bullfrog Books let children practice reading informational text at the earliest reading levels. Repetition, familiar words, and photo labels support early readers.

Before Reading
- Discuss the cover photo. What does it tell them?
- Look at the picture glossary together. Read and discuss the words.

Read the Book
- "Walk" through the book and look at the photos. Let the child ask questions. Point out the photo labels.
- Read the book to the child, or have him or her read independently.

After Reading
- Prompt the child to think more. Ask: Do you like to play in the rain? What sorts of things do you like to do outside when it rains?

Bullfrog Books are published by Jump!
5357 Penn Avenue South
Minneapolis, MN 55419
www.jumplibrary.com

Library of Congress Cataloging-in-Publication Data

Names: Fretland VanVoorst, Jenny, 1972– author.
Title: Rain / by Jenny Fretland VanVoorst.
Description: Minneapolis, MN: Jump!, Inc., [2017]
Series: Weather watch
Audience: Ages 5–8. | Audience: K to grade 3.
Includes bibliographical references and index.
Identifiers: LCCN 2016010930 (print)
LCCN 2016011636 (ebook)
ISBN 9781620313909 (hardcover: alk. paper)
ISBN 9781624964374 (ebook)
Subjects: LCSH: Rain and rainfall—Juvenile literature. | Precipitation (Meteorology)—Juvenile literature. Classification: LCC QC924.7 .F74 2017 (print) | LCC QC924.7 (ebook) | DDC 551.57/7—dc23
LC record available at http://lccn.loc.gov/2016010930

Editor: Kirsten Chang
Series Designer: Ellen Huber
Book Designer: Molly Ballanger
Photo Researcher: Molly Ballanger

Photo Credits: Adobe Stock, 10–11, 12–13, 14, 15, 20–21, 23tl; Getty, 8, 9, 23bl; iStock, 6–7, 18–19, 23tr, 23br; Shutterstock, cover, 1, 5, 16–17, 20–21, 22tr, 24; Thinkstock, 3, 4, 20–21, 22tl, 22bl, 22br.

Printed in the United States of America at Corporate Graphics in North Mankato, Minnesota.

Table of Contents

Let It Rain!

Look up.

What do you see?

Clouds!

How do clouds form?

Water vapor rises.

It sticks to dust
in the air.

vapor

7

The vapor builds up.
It becomes droplets.

droplet

The droplets grow heavy.
They fall to the ground.
Look! It's raining!

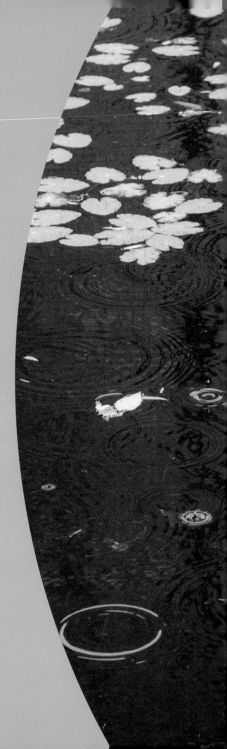

Small drops fall lightly.

A light rain is
called a drizzle.

Large raindrops fall hard.

They make a shower.

We need rain.

Rain feeds plants.

Plants need water to grow.

15

People and animals
need water to live, too.

Rain can be fun.

Mari jumps in a puddle.

It can be comforting.

Listen!

The sound helps
Ty fall asleep.

Good night, rain!

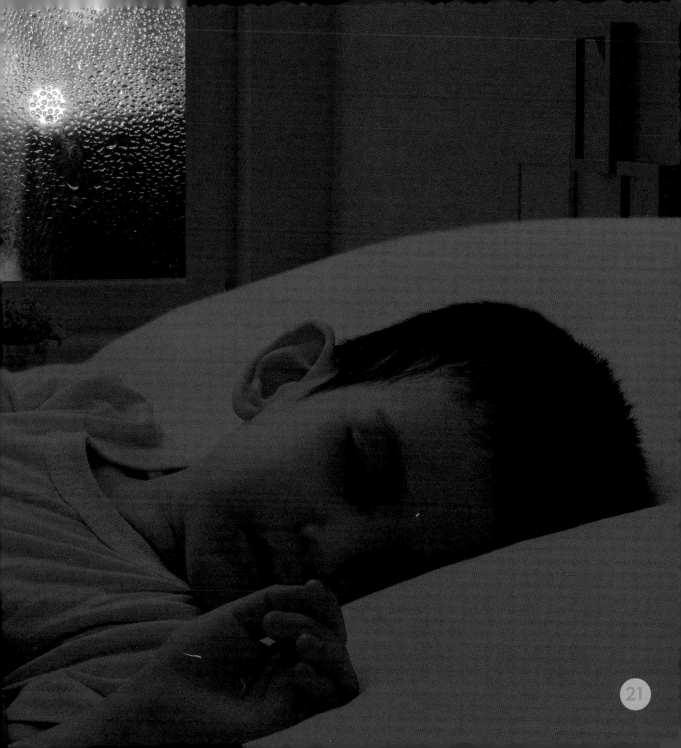

Types of Rainy Weather

sleet
Partially frozen rain.

downpour
A heavy rain.

sprinkle
A light rain.

mist
Water in the form of particles floating in the air or falling as fine rain.

Picture Glossary

drizzle
To rain in very small drops.

puddle
A very small pool of liquid.

droplets
Very small drops.

vapor
Fine particles of a liquid, such as water, that are suspended in the air.

Index

To Learn More

Learning more is as easy as 1, 2, 3.

1) Go to www.factsurfer.com

2) Enter "rain" into the search box.

3) Click the "Surf" button to see a list of websites.

With factsurfer.com, finding more information is just a click away.